THE WORLD'S STUPIDEST
Headlines

Michael O'Mara Humour

First published in Great Britain in 2004 by
Michael O'Mara Books Limited
9 Lion Yard
Tremadoc Road
London SW4 7NQ

A CIP catalogue record for this book is available from the
British Library

ISBN 1-84317-105-8

1 3 5 7 9 10 8 6 4 2

Designed and typeset by Design 23

Printed and bound in Great Britain by Cox & Wyman,
Reading, Berks

THE WORLD'S STUPIDEST
Headlines

INTRODUCTION

Time, or the lack of it, is a crucial factor in the world of newspaper deadlines, but sometimes it pays to take a step back and read the headlines one last time before giving the order to start the presses rolling. Perhaps if more sub-editors had employed a 'more haste, less speed' tactic before submitting their finished copy, then the number and range of stupid headlines selected for this compilation would have been far fewer, and considerably less amusing. Let us be grateful, then, that the pressurized world of newspaper journalism has produced such a wealth of ludicrous headlines which are guaranteed to amuse and entertain.

Containing sections on 'Unintentionally Stupid Headlines' – those which at first glance seem perfectly reasonable, but on closer inspection appear to have ridiculously alternative meanings, e.g. CALIFORNIA GOVERNOR MAKES STAND ON DIRTY TOILETS; 'Stupidly Obvious Headlines' – examples of the most self-evident headlines to have graced a newspaper, including DEAD MAN REMAINS DEAD; 'Bizarrely

Stupid Headlines' – those that have introduced some of the strangest newspaper stories throughout the world, e.g. CHOCOLATE BISCUIT BITES MAN IN MIDNIGHT SNACK ATTACK; and finally 'Stupid Headlines: A Mad Miscellany', devoted to wacky headlines that are simply beyond categorization.

If you happen to spot any other stupid headlines while perusing a local, national or international newspaper, please e-mail them to jokes@michaelomarabooks.com, for possible inclusion in future collections.

Unintentionally Stupid Headlines

4-H Girls Win Prizes For Fat Calves

Workers Finish Boring Sewer Tunnel

Transsexuals Benefits Cut Off

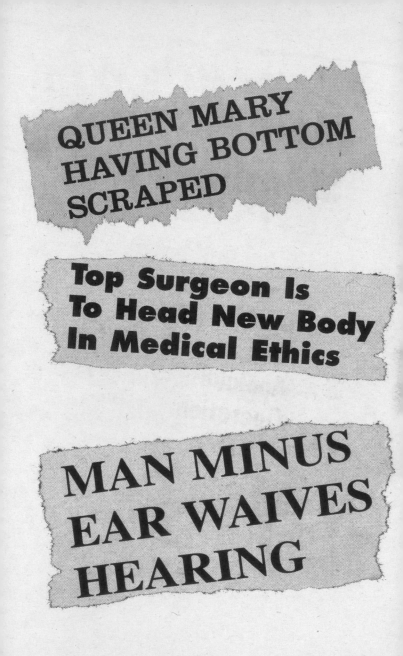

Male Naturist Members Rise

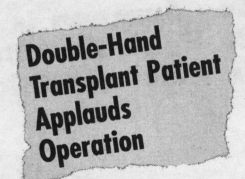

Double-Hand Transplant Patient Applauds Operation

Eunuchs Strut Their Stuff On Indian Catwalk

Doctor Testifies In Horse Suit

Crematorium Plans Put On Back Burner

Lesotho Women Make Great Carpets

JUVENILE COURT TO TRY SHOOTING DEFENDANT

'Gunproof' Chief Shot

FALSE CHARGE OF THEFT OF HENS
Police On Wild Goose Chase

HOSPITALS ARE SUED BY 7 FOOT DOCTORS

Lingerie Shipment Hijacked – Thief Gives Police The Slip

CRASH COURSES FOR PRIVATE PILOTS

MAN STRUCK BY LIGHTNING FACES BATTERY CHARGE

One-legged Man Competent To Stand Trial

PROSECUTOR RELEASES PROBE INTO UNDERSHERIFF

Patient At Death's Door — Doctors Pull Him Through

SHOT OFF WOMAN'S LEG HELPS NICKLAUS TO 66

Giant Waves Down Queen Mary's Funnel

DRUNK GETS NINE MONTHS IN VIOLIN CASE

Clinton Stiff On Withdrawal

MORE WOMEN NEEDED FOR RANDOM SAMPLING

Mrs Rydell's Bust Unveiled At Nearby School

Invisible Man Disappears From View

Golfers Warned Not To Lick Balls

Cocaine Use Hits New High

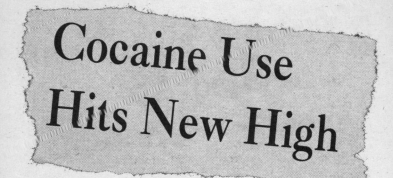

Golfer Charged With Drunken Driving

Caribbean Islands Drift To Left

10 Revolting Officers Executed

ASTRONAUT TAKES BLAME FOR GAS IN SPACECRAFT

General Eisenhower Flies Back To Front

BLIND BISHOP APPOINTED TO SEE

Antique Stripper To Display Wares At Store

MASSIVE ORGAN DRAWS THE CROWD

Alzheimer's Centre Prepares For An Affair To Remember

20-Year Friendship Ends At Altar

Council To Stamp On Dog Mess

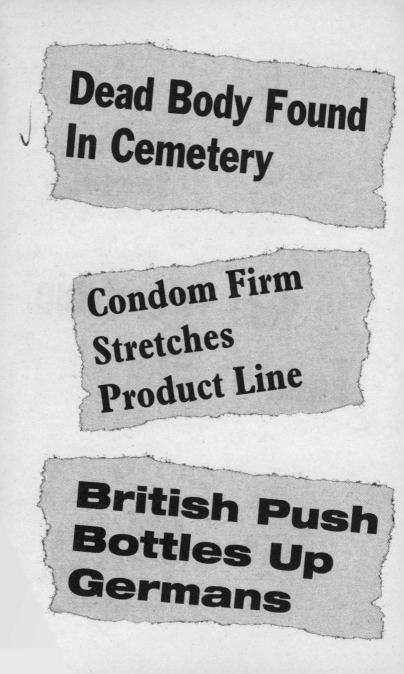

Dead Body Found In Cemetery

Condom Firm Stretches Product Line

British Push Bottles Up Germans

INCLUDE YOUR CHILDREN WHEN BAKING COOKIES

LA Voters Approve Urban Renewal By Landslide

MAN SHOOTS NEIGHBOUR WITH MACHETE

Drugs Runner Hid Crack In His Pants

FILMING IN CEMETERY ANGERS RESIDENTS

Manure Management Effort Makes A Splash At Ag Expo

Ancient Blonde Corpses Raise Questions

Flaming Toilet Seat Causes Evacuation At High School

Defendant's Speech Ends In Long Sentence

Invisible Man Comes Out Of Hiding

BLIND WOMAN GETS NEW KIDNEY FROM DAD SHE HASN'T SEEN IN YEARS

Judge To Rule On Nude Beach

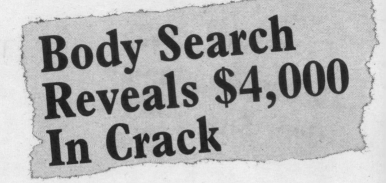

Body Search Reveals $4,000 In Crack

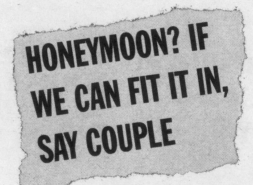

HONEYMOON? IF WE CAN FIT IT IN, SAY COUPLE

Man Eating Piranha Mistakenly Sold As Pet Fish

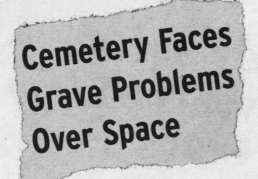

Cemetery Faces Grave Problems Over Space

BISHOP HOISTS HIS CASSOCK TO REVEAL A SECRET

LIMBLESS HIT OUT AT RISE IN LIVING COSTS

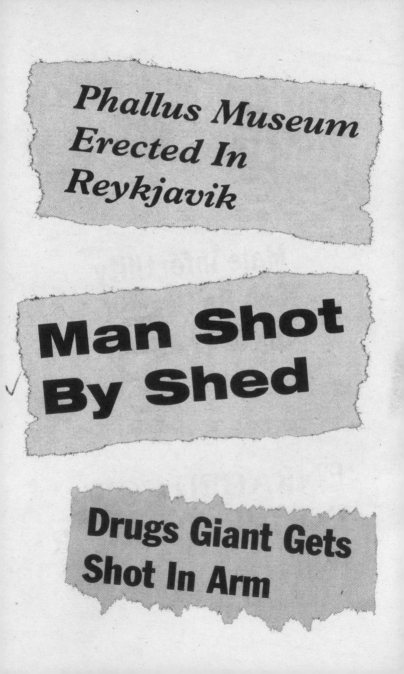

BANK DRIVE-IN WINDOW BLOCKED BY BOARD

Male Infertility Can Be Passed On To Children

ENRAGED COW INJURES FARMER WITH AXE

Lawyers Give Poor Free Legal Advice

SOVIET VIRGIN LANDS SHORT OF GOAL AGAIN

Passengers Hit by Cancelled Trains

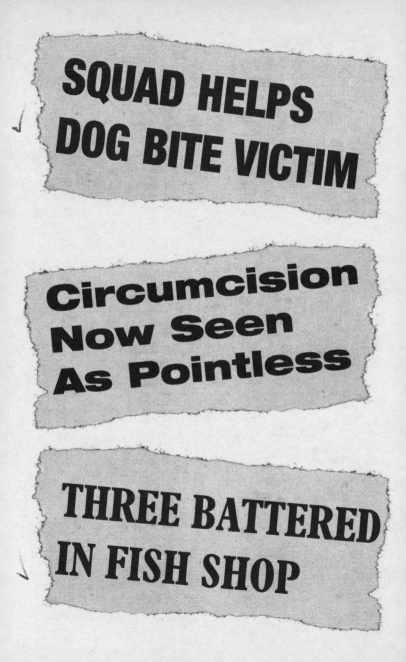

Thugs Eat Then Rob Proprietor

Clinton's Firmness Got Results

STOLEN PAINTING FOUND BY TREE

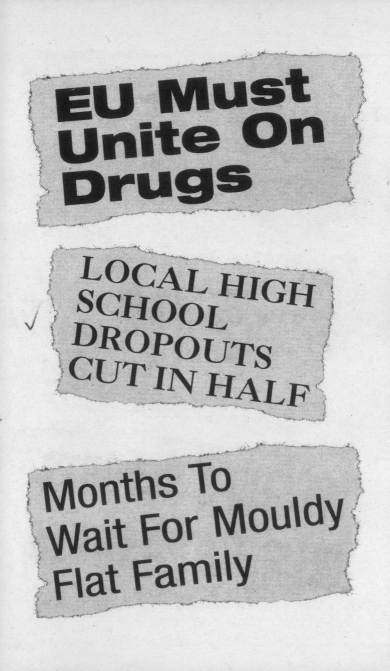

EU Must Unite On Drugs

LOCAL HIGH SCHOOL DROPOUTS CUT IN HALF

Months To Wait For Mouldy Flat Family

TYPHOON RIPS THROUGH CEMETERY; HUNDREDS DEAD

China Drag Queens Have Officials On Their Knees

WEATHER REPORTS DEPRESS POTATOES

Governor Chiles Offers Rare Opportunity To Goose Hunters

SPARE OUR TREES— THEY BREAK WIND

Textron Inc. Makes Offer To Screw Company Stockholders

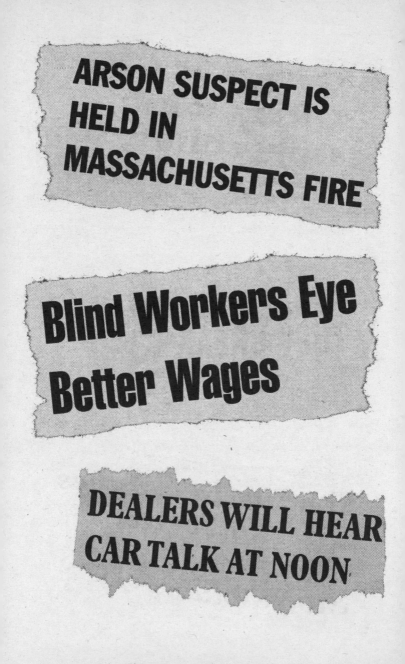

ARSON SUSPECT IS HELD IN MASSACHUSETTS FIRE

Blind Workers Eye Better Wages

DEALERS WILL HEAR CAR TALK AT NOON

Heart Failure Classes Planned

Hooked On Internet? Help Is Just A Click Away

Frozen Semen Talks

**Dog Dirt In Park
– Group Leaders
Step In**

**GRANDMOTHER OF EIGHT
MAKES HOLE IN ONE**

**Experts Test
16,000
Condoms**

Gunman Shot
By 999 Cops

NEW STUDY OF OBESITY LOOKS
FOR LARGER TEST GROUP

Marijuana Issue
Sent To A Joint
Committee

Drug Abuse 'Can Be Beaten By Joint Effort'

HOUSE PASSES GAS TAX ON TO SENATE

Magician's Car Vanishes

POLICE BEGIN CAMPAIGN TO RUN DOWN JAYWALKERS

Sex Scandal Vicar Seeks New Position

ORGAN FESTIVAL ENDS IN SMASHING CLIMAX

PROSTITUTES APPEAL TO POPE

Woman Is Pregnant Thanks To Her Sister

TWO SOVIET SHIPS COLLIDE – ONE DIES

Portable Toilet Bombed, Police Have Nothing To Go On

OUR WOMEN LICK MALE SPORTSMEN

Use Of Heroin Shooting Up

RED TAPE HOLDS UP NEW BRIDGE

Officers Shoot Dead Burglar In Siege

PROTESTOR TRIES TO SPOIL PLAY BUT THE ACTORS SUCCEEDED

Nurses Warn Against Rash Use Of Herbal Oil Treatments

IS THERE A RING OF DEBRIS AROUND URANUS?

Surgery For Duck Hurt By Anglers Left Hook

Fund Set Up For Beating Victim's Kin

SURVIVOR OF SIAMESE TWINS JOINS PARENTS

Iowa Cemeteries Are Death Traps

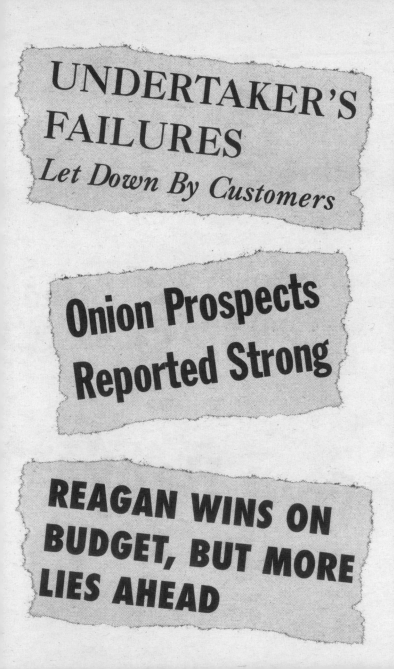

UNDERTAKER'S FAILURES
Let Down By Customers

Onion Prospects Reported Strong

REAGAN WINS ON BUDGET, BUT MORE LIES AHEAD

Jerk Injures Neck, Wins Award

'Missing' WPC Found Weeping In Panda

Foot Heads Arms Body

Lucky Man Sees Friends Die

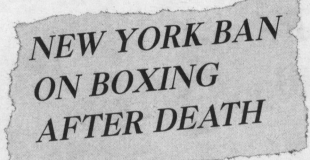

NEW YORK BAN ON BOXING AFTER DEATH

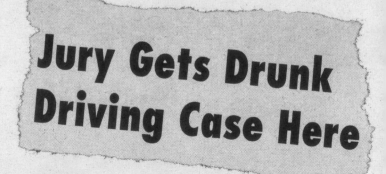

Jury Gets Drunk Driving Case Here

MOUNTING PROBLEMS FOR YOUNG COUPLES

Ribena Offer To Blood Service

Police Discover Crack In Australia

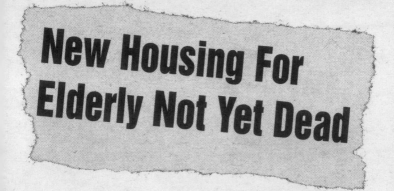

New Housing For Elderly Not Yet Dead

SEX EDUCATION DELAYED, TEACHERS REQUEST TRAINING

Top Surgeon Is To Head New Body In Medical Ethics

Tiny Babies Do Worse In Exams

Men Get A Lesson On Kerb Crawling

Pupils Train As Counsellors To Help Upset Classmates

Victim Tied, Nude Policeman Testifies

Passengers To Wait 10 Years For Fast Trains

S. Florida Illegal Aliens Cut In Half By New Law

TWO SISTERS REUNITED AFTER 18 YEARS AT CHECKOUT COUNTER

Prostitutes To Hold Open Day

Nickers Leave Hospital Crutchless

MAD COW TALKS

Two One-Legged Inmates Skip Jail

Genetic Engineering Splits Scientists

SAFETY EXPERTS SAY SCHOOL BUS PASSENGERS SHOULD BE BELTED

Undergrads Flunk Sperm Bank Tests

PANDA MATING FAILS; VETERINARIAN TAKES OVER

CIA Drafts Covert Plan to Topple Saddam

KIDS MAKE NUTRITIOUS SNACKS

Let The People Decide On Drugs

Cops Quiz Victim In Fatal Shooting

HERSHEY BARS PROTEST

Arafat Swears In Cabinet

Columnist Gets Urologist In Trouble With His Peers

AUTOS KILLING 110 A DAY, LET'S RESOLVE TO DO BETTER

Family Of 17 Defects From North Korea

Bridge Sets 60 Mph Limit For Pedestrians

Gorillas Of Rwanda Lecture At Museum Of Natural History

Circumcisions Cause Crybabies

BRITISH LEFT WAFFLES ON FALKLAND ISLANDS

Watchdog Gets A New Head

STRIPPED GIRL, Yard To Probe

TWO CONVICTS EVADE NOOSE, JURY HUNG

Body Wants New Blood

STIFF OPPOSITION EXPECTED TO CASKETLESS FUNERAL PLAN

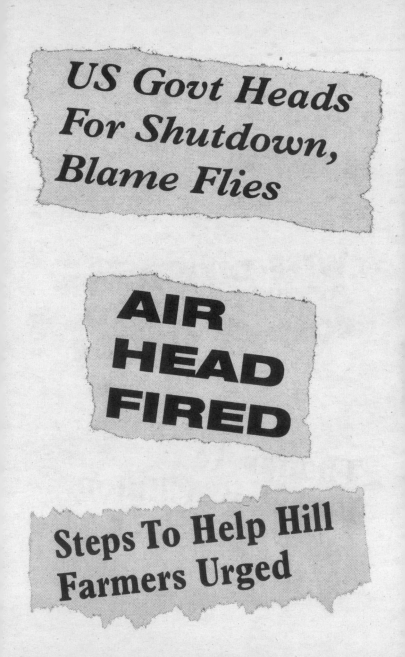

US Govt Heads
For Shutdown,
Blame Flies

AIR
HEAD
FIRED

Steps To Help Hill
Farmers Urged

Briton Gored By Bull In Intensive Care

WIFE DIED AFTER ATTEMPTING TO COMMIT SUICIDE

Thanks To President Clinton, Staff Sgt Fruer Now Has A Son

Mrs Corson's Seat Up For Grabs

PRISONERS ESCAPE AFTER EXECUTION

Town To Drop School Bus, When Overpass Is Ready

SHELL FOUND ON BEACH

Police: Body Cavity Search Reveals Crack

EYE DROPS OFF SHELF

Largest Amount Of Cannabis Ever Seized In Joint Operation

SMOKERS ARE PRODUCTIVE, BUT DEATH CUTS EFFICIENCY

Phantom Actor Sues

MINERS REFUSE TO WORK AFTER DEATH

US Food Service, Feeds Thousands, Grosses Millions

QUARTER OF A MILLION CHINESE LIVE ON WATER

NEVER WITHHOLD HERPES INFECTION FROM LOVED ONE

Jane Fonda To Teens: Use Head To Avoid Pregnancy

DR RUTH TO TALK ABOUT SEX WITH NEWSPAPER EDITORS

Lack Of Brains Hinders Research

Man With One Arm And Leg Cheats On Other Half

Penile Implants Raise Hopes

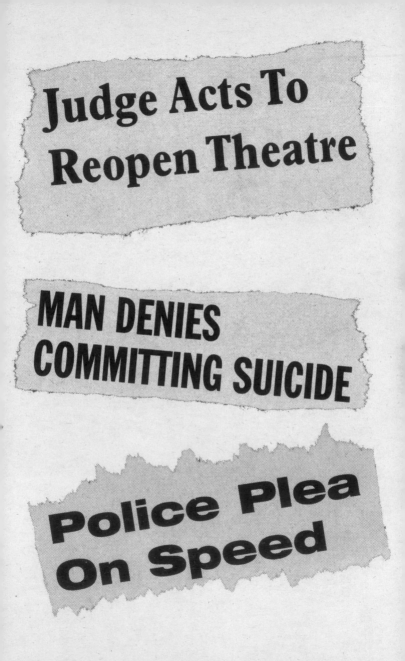

Judge Acts To Reopen Theatre

MAN DENIES COMMITTING SUICIDE

Police Plea On Speed

MILK DRINKERS ARE TURNING TO POWDER

Home Secretary To Act On Video Nasties

PORTERS MARCH OVER ASIAN IMMIGRANTS

Man Steals Clock, Faces Time

NICARAGUA SETS GOAL TO WIPE OUT LITERACY

Statistics Show That Teen Pregnancy Drops Off Significantly After Age 25

OLD SCHOOL PILLARS ARE REPLACED BY ALUMNI

SMALL ORGANS TRENDY

Man Shot In Los Boliches

TIGER WOODS PLAYS WITH OWN BALLS, NIKE SAYS

Nuns Drop Suit; Bishops Agree To Aid Them

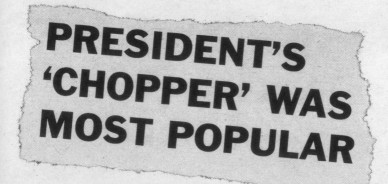

PRESIDENT'S 'CHOPPER' WAS MOST POPULAR

NY Ponders Beating Victim

POLICE MOVE IN BOOK CASE

Man Steals Car To Get To Car Theft Hearing

Cuts Could Hurt Animals

THREATENING LETTERS – MAN ASKS FOR LONG SENTENCE

Diaper Market Bottoms Out

Sex Fund Pledged For Sheriff

DEAF MUTE GETS NEW HEARING IN KILLING

Man Recovering After Fatal Accident

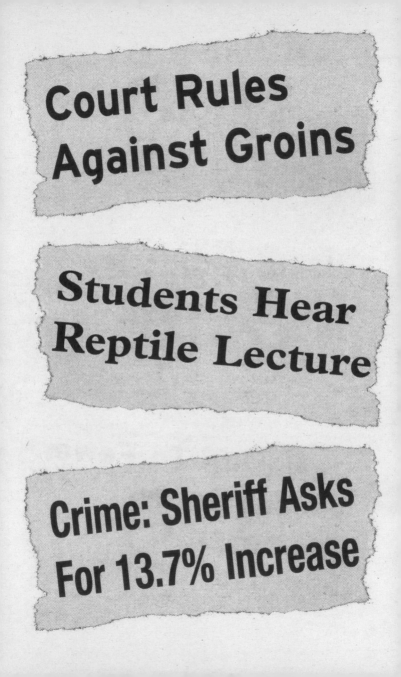

Court Rules
Against Groins

Students Hear
Reptile Lecture

Crime: Sheriff Asks
For 13.7% Increase

Clinton Places Dickey In Gore's Hands

12 ON THEIR WAY TO CRUISE AMONG DEAD IN PLANE CRASH

Downside To Fewer Violent Deaths: Transplant Organ Shortage Grows

City Pact Fight Boils

NEW VACCINE MAY CONTAIN RABIES

Body Found On Boat Seized By Bailiffs And Due To Be Auctioned

DRUNK DRIVERS PAID $1,000 IN 1984

Police Seek Witnesses To Assault

LUNG CANCER IN WOMEN MUSHROOMS

Bulge In Trousers Was Ecstasy

Mayor Bans SEX At Local Library

Drug Dealers Dealt Heavy Blow Say Police

STRIP CLUB SHOCK, Magistrates May Act On Indecent Shows

Save Streams, Fish Head Warns

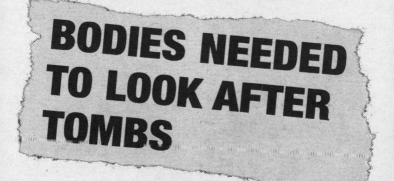

BODIES NEEDED TO LOOK AFTER TOMBS

Complaints About NBA Referees Growing Ugly

END TO FREE SCHOOL LOOMS

Axe For Media School's Head

California Governor Makes Stand On Dirty Toilets

CHEF THROWS HIS HEART INTO HELPING FEED NEEDY

Former Python To Open Giraffe House

Bush Orders Army Troops To US Virgins

BRITISH UNION FINDS DWARFS IN SHORT SUPPLY

Celibacy Could Make Priests Extinct

Cancer Society Honours Marlboro Man

COUNCIL 'DIGGING OWN GRAVE', Smaller Body Urged

Bull's Sperm Comes Under The Hammer

Stupidly Obvious Headlines

Ability To Swim May Save Children From Drowning

Dead Man Remains Dead

Fish Lurk In Streams

Ferries Must Stay Afloat In Worst Of Storms, Say Safety Engineers

Bad Driving Causes Most Car Crashes

Alcohol Ads Promote Drinking

Bible Church's Focus Is The Bible

Foul Play Suspected In Death Of Man Found Handless, Bound And Hanged

More Exercise May Help Weight Loss

COLD WAVE LINKED TO TEMPERATURES

Jail Crowding Caused By Increase In Criminals, New Study Concludes

PSYCHICS PREDICT WORLD DIDN'T END YESTERDAY

Larger Kangaroos Leap Farther, Researchers Find

ENFIELD COUPLE SLAIN; POLICE SUSPECT HOMICIDE

Sneak Attack By Soviet Bloc Not Foreseen

IF STRIKE ISN'T SETTLED QUICKLY, IT MAY LAST A WHILE

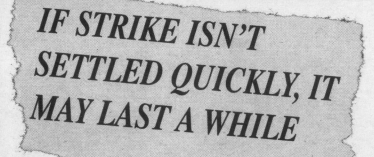

Plenty of Sex Advised for Successful Pregnancy

PLANE TOO CLOSE TO GROUND, CRASH PROBE TOLD

Official: Only Rain Will Cure Drought

Farmers Buy Most Farmland

Dirty-Air Cities Far Deadlier Than Clean Ones, Study Shows

Smaller Families Require Less Food

SOMETHING WENT WRONG IN JET CRASH, EXPERT SAYS

Collapsed Bridge In China Faulty

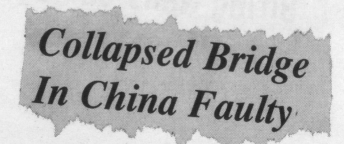

Bad Food Makes
A Poor Picnic

Scientists See
Quakes In L.A. Future

Biting Nails Can Be
Sign Of Tenseness
In A Person

Survey Finds Dirtier Subways After Cleaning Jobs Were Cut

WAR DIMS HOPE FOR PEACE

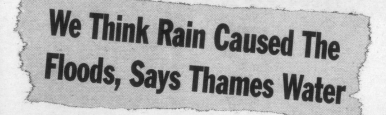

We Think Rain Caused The Floods, Says Thames Water

Study Finds That Pupils Who Attend Their Classes Score Markedly Better

Fatal Mudslide Blamed On Hill

Artificial Intelligence Like Real Thing

Bizarrely Stupid Headlines

Jury Clears Cow In Car Accident

Man Tossing Knife In The Air Stabs Self In Head

40 Men Escape Watery Graves When Vessel Flounders In Ale

No Cause Of Death Determined For Beheading Victim

KILLER SENTENCED TO DIE FOR SECOND TIME IN 10 YEARS

Hundreds Hurt During Stone-throwing Festival

Lawyer Says Client Is Not That Guilty

Bananas And Oranges Linked To Violent Crime

Police Kill Youth In Effort To Stop His Suicide Attempt

National Slacker Day May Be Too Much Effort

Alien Hedgehogs Spread Terror In The Hebrides

Chocolate Biscuit Bites Man In Midnight Snack Attack

Baker Stabbed Woman 99 Times In Self-Defence

Airborne Deer Kills Man

Legislator Wants Tougher Death Penalty

Dead Golfer Plays His Best Round

French Police Suspect Nudist Site Has Something to Hide

Fisherman Arrested For Using Wife As Shark Bait

Airline Travel Safer Despite More Accidents

El Nino Blamed For Rise In Diarrhoea In Peru

Council Informs Woman Who Died Two Years Ago She Is Dead

Man Jumps Off 2nd Street Bridge; Neither Jumper Nor Body Found

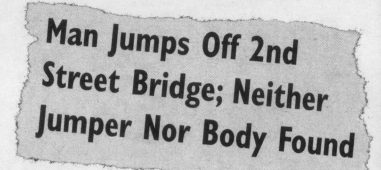

Gas Smell Diverts Flight, But It Was Just Passengers Pants

Pilot Vows To Quit Flying After Landing On His Wife

Groin Kick Led To 7-Day Erection

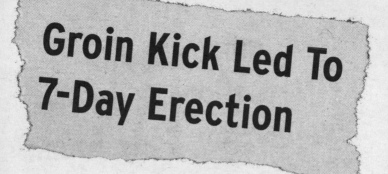

News Crew Pickpocketed While Covering Pickpocket Story

Spaniard Hits Girlfriend At Anti-Violence Rally

Americans Driven To Suicide By Fear Of Death

Crazed Elephant Found In Sea

Train Driver Temporarily Blinded By Exploding Pigeon

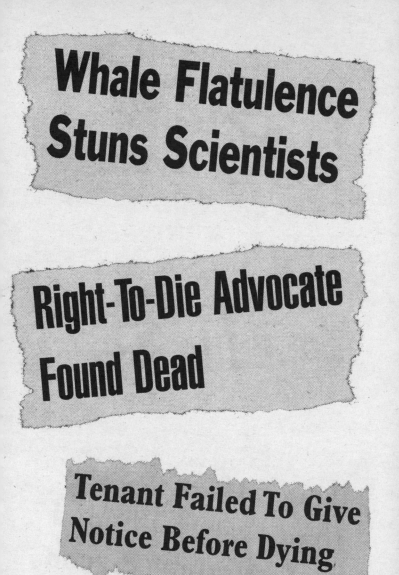

W.I. To Remove Jam From Toilets

Man Goes Berserk In Car Saleroom, Many Volvos Hurt

Nude Scene Done Tastefully In Radio Play

Toy Gun Scares
Robber Using Toy Gun

Mimes Blamed For
Abusive Language

More Men Found
Wedded Than Women

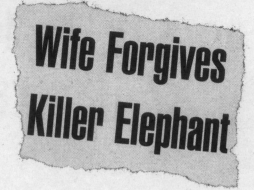

Wife Forgives Killer Elephant

Teacher Dies; Board Accepts His Resignation

'Save The Whales' Trip Cut Short After Boat Rams Whale

Water Missing In The Middle Of The Sea

Youth Hit By Train Is Rushed To Two Hospitals

Sand Found On Beach Shocker

Local Man Has Longest Horns In Texas

Race Cyclists Caught Speeding

Greek Bars Close Early In Protest At Early Closure

FATHER OF TEN SHOT DEAD, Mistaken For Rabbit

Lawyer Frees Own Killer

DEAD POLICEMAN IN THE FORCE FOR 18 YEARS

Cow Attacks School Cook

Mayor Says D.C. Is Safe Except For Murders

Church Goes Missing

Stupid Headlines: A Mad Miscellany

VOLUNTARY WORKERS STRIKE FOR HIGHER PAY

Man On Singles Holiday Finds Himself Alone

MINE STRIKE BALLET TO GO AHEAD

US Audit Finds Funds For Youth Misspent

Cash Plea To Help Dyslexic Cildren

Henman Sees Balls As Key To His Success

5 Scientists Study Cancer Risks Of Grilling, Flying, Unprotected Sex

Tarzan's Loincloth Hid A Big Swinger

Brain Bank Seeks More Deposits

Flying Fanny Thrills Thousands

The former Dutch sprinter FANNY BLANKERS-KOEN, who died in January 2004, was known as the Flying Housewife, and was named as the greatest woman athlete of the twentieth century for a string of world records and four gold medals in the 1948 Olympics. This unforgettable *Evening News* headline greeted her on a visit to Scotland.

Bonnie Blows Clinton

In August 1998, Hurricane Bonnie's flight through Clinton, North Carolina, knocked out power cables and caused chaos in the area.

Big Ugly Woman Wins Beauty Pageant

This headline appeared in a local newspaper in the town of Big Ugly, West Virginia.

All Michael O'Mara titles are available by post from:

Bookpost, PO Box 29, Douglas, Isle of Man, IM99 1BQ

Credit cards accepted.
Telephone: 01624 677237
Fax: 01624 670923
Email: bookshop@enterprise.net
Internet: www.bookpost.co.uk

Free postage and packing in the UK.

Other Michael O'Mara Humour titles:

The Book of Urban Legends – ISBN 1-85479-932-0 pb £3.99
Born for the Job – ISBN 1-84317-099-X pb £5.99
The Complete Book of Farting – ISBN 1-85479-440-X pb £4.99
The Ultimate Insult – ISBN 1-85479-288-1 pb £5.99
Wicked Cockney Rhyming Slang – ISBN 1-85479-386-1 pb £3.99
The Wicked Wit of Jane Austen – ISBN 1-85479-652-6 hb £9.99
The Wicked Wit of Winston Churchill – ISBN 1-85479-529-5 hb £9.99
The Wicked Wit of Oscar Wilde – ISBN 1-85479-542-2 hb £9.99
The World's Stupidest Laws – ISBN 1-85479-549-X pb £3.99
The World's Stupidest Signs – ISBN 1-85479-555-4 pb £3.99
More of the World's Stupidest Signs – ISBN 1-84317-032-9 pb £4.99
The World's Stupidest Last Words – ISBN 1-84317-021-3 pb £4.99
The World's Stupidest Inventions – ISBN 1-84317-036-1 pb £5.99
The World's Stupidest Instructions – ISBN 1-84317-078-7 pb £4.99
The World's Stupidest Sporting Screw-Ups – ISBN 1-84317-039-6 pb £4.99
Shite's Unoriginal Miscellany – ISBN 1-84317-064-7 hb £9.99
Cricket: It's A Funny Old Game – ISBN 1-84317-090-6 pb £4.99
Football: It's A Funny Old Game – ISBN 1-84317-091-4 pb £4.99
Laughable Latin – ISBN 1-84317-097-3 pb £4.99
School Rules – ISBN 1-84317-100-7 pb £4.99
Sex Cheques (new edition) – ISBN 1-84317-121-X pb £3.50
Eats, Shites & Leaves – ISBN 1-84317-098-1 hb £9.99
The Timewaster Letters – ISBN 1-84317-108-2 pb £9.99
The Jordan Joke Book – ISBN 1-84317-120-1 pb £4.99
Speak Well English – ISBN 1-84317-088-4 pb £5.99